THE GREATEST
FOOTBALL PLAYERS
OF ALL TIME

Gareth Stevens
PUBLISHING

BY MATTHEW JANKOWSKI

Please visit our website, www.garethstevens.com. For a free color catalog of all our high-quality books, call toll free 1-800-542-2595 or fax 1-877-542-2596.

Library of Congress Cataloging-in-Publication Data

Names: Jankowski, Matthew, author.
Title: The greatest football players of all time / Matthew Jankowski.
Description: New York : Gareth Stevens Publishing, 2020. | Series: Greatest of all time. Sports stars | Includes index. | Contents: Come Join the Huddle – Quarterback Joe "Joe Cool" Montana – Quarterback Johnny"Johnny U" Unitas – Quarterback John Elway – Running back Jim Brown – Running back Walter "Sweetness" Payton – Wide receiver Jerry Rice – Tight end Tony Gonzalez – Offensive line Anthony Munoz – Defensive line Reggie White – Linebacker Lawrence Taylor – Defensive back Ronnie Lott – Future record breakers – Glossary.
Identifiers: LCCN 2019027318 | ISBN 9781538247792 (paperback) | ISBN 9781538247808 | ISBN 9781538247815 (library binding) | ISBN 9781538247822 (ebook)
Subjects: LCSH: Football players–United States–Biography–Juvenile literature.
Classification: LCC GV939.A1 J36 2020 | DDC 796.3320922–dc23
LC record available at https://lccn.loc.gov/2019027318

First Edition

Published in 2020 by
Gareth Stevens Publishing
111 East 14th Street, Suite 349
New York, NY 10003

Designer: Katelyn E. Reynolds
Editor: Emily Mahoney

Photo credits: Cover, p. 1 Stacy Revere/Getty Images; cover, pp. 1–32 (series art) Dmitry Kostrov/ Shutterstock.com; cover, pp. 1–32 (series background) rangizzz/Shutterstock.com; pp. 5, 29 (football graphic) johavel/Shutterstock.com; pp. 7, 9, 12, 13, 14, 15, 17, 20, 23, 25, 27 Focus on Sport/Getty Images; p. 11 Tim DeFrisco/Allsport/Getty Images; p. 19 Mike Ehrmann/Getty Images; pp. 21, 24 Peter Brouillet/Getty Images; p. 22 MATTCAMPBELL/AFP/Getty Images; p. 28 Christian Petersen/ Getty Images.

Printed in the United States of America

CPSIA compliance information: Batch #CW20GS: For further information contact Gareth Stevens, New York, New York at 1-800-542-2595.

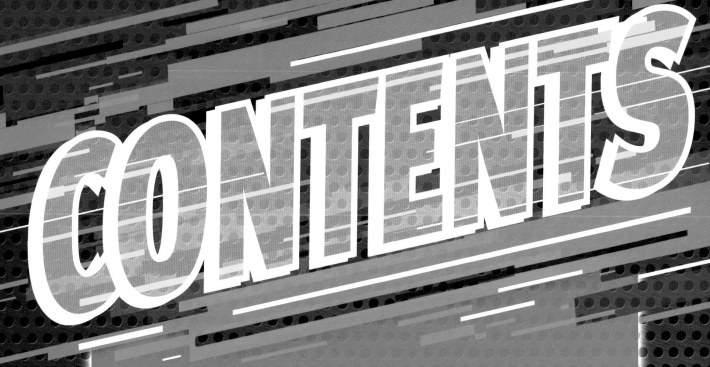

CONTENTS

WORDS IN THE GLOSSARY APPEAR IN BOLD TEXT THE FIRST TIME THEY ARE USED IN THE TEXT.

COME JOIN THE HUDDLE

Hut, hut, hike! Maybe you picked up this guide to the greatest football players of all time because you want to learn more about the sport, or maybe you are an up-and-coming football star yourself! Well, if you want to learn more, then why not learn from the best?

This book will let you explore the careers of some of the greatest players ever to play the game of football. From offensive athletes, who could not be stopped, to defenders, who gave opponents nightmares, here are eleven players who passed, ran, caught, tackled, and blocked better than everyone else.

4 LEGENDARY PLAYS THROUGHOUT NFL HISTORY

HAIL MARY	ON THE LAST PLAY OF THE GAME, THE QUARTERBACK SAYS A PRAYER AND THROWS THE BALL AS FAR AS HE CAN. PROBABLY THE MOST FAMOUS HAIL MARY PLAY WAS THE IMMACULATE RECEPTION, WHERE RUNNING BACK FRANCO HARRIS OF THE PITTSBURGH STEELERS HAULED IN A TIPPED BOMB TO SCORE THE WINNING TOUCHDOWN.
FUMBLEROOSKI	THE QUARTERBACK RECEIVES THE SNAP AND INTENTIONALLY LEAVES THE BALL ON THE GROUND AS A FUMBLE, PRETENDING TO STILL BE LOOKING TO PASS. SOMEONE ELSE ON THE OFFENSE PICKS UP THE BALL AND RUNS THROUGH THE DEFENSE SECRETLY! BELIEVE IT OR NOT, THIS PLAY HAS ACTUALLY WORKED.
HOOK AND LADDER	A PLAY WHERE ONE WIDE RECEIVER CATCHES A PASS AND LATERALS OR THROWS IT BACKWARDS TO ANOTHER RECEIVER TO KEEP THE PLAY ALIVE.
STATUE OF LIBERTY PLAY	A TRICK PLAY TO FOOL THE DEFENSE, THE QUARTERBACK PRETENDS TO THROW A QUICK PASS, BUT KEEPS THE BALL BEHIND HIS BACK, SECRETLY KEEPING IT TO RUN HIMSELF, OR SNEAKILY HANDOFF TO SOMEONE ELSE.

MANY FOOTBALL PLAYERS BECOME FAMOUS BECAUSE THEY MAKE BIG PLAYS, SUCH AS SCORING OR THROWING A TOUCHDOWN. HERE ARE SOME EXAMPLES OF SOME UNBELIEVEABLE THINGS THAT THE PLAYERS IN THIS BOOK HAVE DONE!

BE A STUDENT OF THE GAME

THIS BOOK IS MEANT TO BE AN INTRODUCTION TO THE GREATEST FOOTBALL PLAYERS. IF YOU FIND YOU ADMIRE AN ATHLETE MENTIONED IN THIS BOOK, YOU CAN ALWAYS LEARN MORE ABOUT THEM. THERE IS MUCH MORE INFORMATION OUT THERE TO READ AND TO WATCH, SO YOU CAN START YOUR OWN FOOTBALL JOURNEY TOO!

QUARTERBACK
JOE "JOE COOL" MONTANA

Joe Montana is known for winning, simple as that. He led the San Francisco 49ers to four Super Bowls and they won every single one. Even in college, Joe went from seventh-string quarterback to winning a National Championship in 1977. He was selected in the third round of the 1979 NFL draft.

"Joe Cool" proved he was an accurate passer who could **scramble** to keep plays alive. He earned two most valuable player (MVP) awards and was selected to play in the Pro Bowl eight times. When he **retired** after 16 years, Joe Montana held records for completed passes, yards passing, and touchdowns during the playoffs.

JOE MONTANA THREW FOR 273 TOUCHDOWNS, OVER 40,000 YARDS, AND HAD A 92.3 PASSER RATING ACROSS HIS CAREER. HE WAS INDUCTED INTO THE NFL HALL OF FAME IN 2000.

COOL AS THE OTHER SIDE OF THE PILLOW

JOE MONTANA PLAYED AT THE QUARTERBACK POSITION. QUARTERBACKS ARE NOT ONLY RESPONSIBLE FOR THROWING PASSES, BUT ALSO FOR READING DEFENSES AND CONTROLLING THE PACE OF THE GAME. MONTANA EARNED THE NICKNAME "JOE COOL" BECAUSE OF HIS ABILITY TO REMAIN CALM UNDER PRESSURE AND LEAD HIS TEAM TO VICTORY IN THE FINAL MOMENTS OF A GAME.

QUARTERBACK
JOHNNY "JOHNNY U" UNITAS

Johnny Unitas played professional football for 18 years and every year, he managed to **exceed** everyone's expectations for him. Johnny U was not drafted into the NFL until the ninth round (out of 17). He was cut from the Pittsburgh Steelers before the Colts picked him up. Johnny Unitas wanted to prove himself, and he did!

Unitas was known for his confidence, courage, leadership, play-calling, and accurate passes. Johnny U threw for at least one touchdown in 47 games straight! He was player of the year three times, won the Super Bowl, and was chosen for the NFL Hall of Fame.

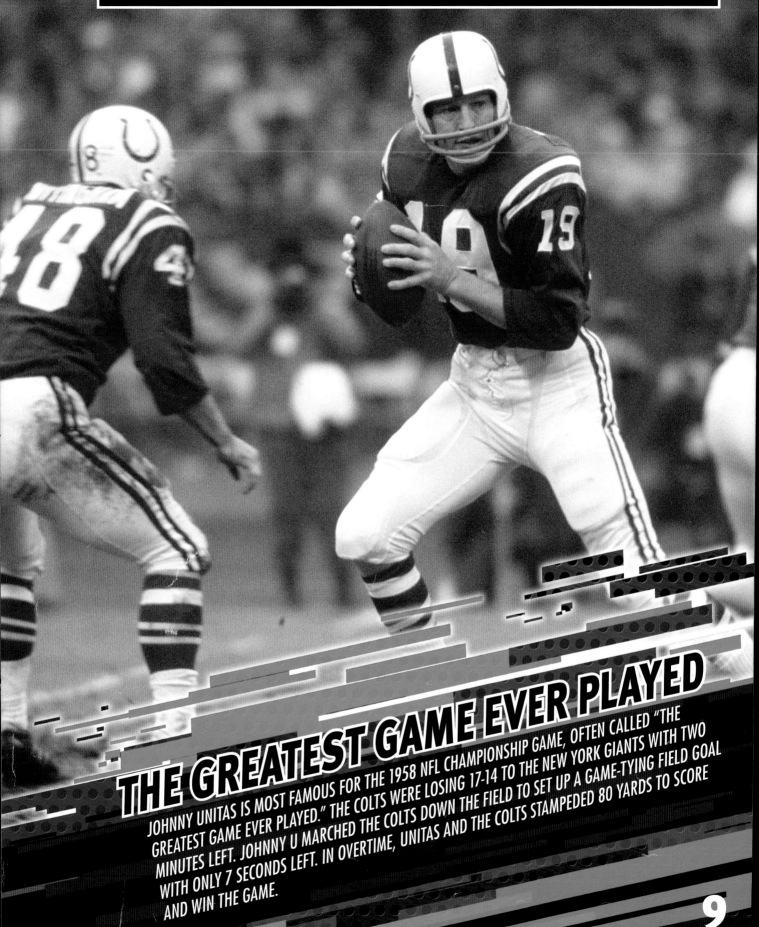

THE GREATEST GAME EVER PLAYED

JOHNNY UNITAS IS MOST FAMOUS FOR THE 1958 NFL CHAMPIONSHIP GAME, OFTEN CALLED "THE GREATEST GAME EVER PLAYED." THE COLTS WERE LOSING 17-14 TO THE NEW YORK GIANTS WITH TWO MINUTES LEFT. JOHNNY U MARCHED THE COLTS DOWN THE FIELD TO SET UP A GAME-TYING FIELD GOAL WITH ONLY 7 SECONDS LEFT. IN OVERTIME, UNITAS AND THE COLTS STAMPEDED 80 YARDS TO SCORE AND WIN THE GAME.

QUARTERBACK
JOHN ELWAY

John Elway had every **asset** needed to become one of the greatest quarterbacks ever. Elway could launch the ball deep, thread the needle with shorter passes, and keep plays alive with his feet. Elway passed for over 3,000 yards and ran for more than 200 yards in seven straight seasons. He played for 16 years, scoring 334 touchdowns, playing in nine Pro Bowls, and winning four Super Bowls.

Elway was also known for smiling when under pressure. He has a record 47 game-winning or game-tying drives in the fourth quarter. This includes a 98-yard come-from-behind scoring drive late in a 1986 playoff game that has become remembered simply as "The Drive."

IT'S ALMOST IMPOSSIBLE TO PICTURE JOHN ELWAY WITHOUT THE DENVER BRONCOS' FAMOUS ORANGE AND BLUE JERSEY. ELWAY STUCK WITH LUCKY 7 AS HIS NUMBER FOR HIS WHOLE CAREER.

SUCKING WIND?

POSSIBLY THE MOST IMPRESSIVE PART OF ELWAY'S ACCOMPLISHMENTS IS THAT HE PLAYED IN DENVER. DENVER'S STADIUM, CALLED MILE HIGH STADIUM, IS AT A HIGH **ELEVATION** POINT WHICH CAN LEAD TO BREATHING DIFFICULTIES. YOU TRULY HAVE TO BE IN SHAPE TO PLAY WELL THERE!

RUNNING BACK

JIM BROWN

Jim Brown played for the Cleveland Browns, and he was one of the greats because of his amazing strength, speed, and intelligence. Cleveland was **fortunate** to have him on their team. Jim Brown played for nine seasons and made it to the Pro Bowl every single year.

Jim Brown did it all. He was top of the league in the 1960s with his running yards, he returned kickoffs, and he even threw three touchdown passes. Jim's hard work and **dedication** paid off as the Cleveland Browns won the championship in 1964!

CAN YOU SAY INVINCIBLE?

JIM BROWN IS ONE OF THE MOST IMPRESSIVE ATHLETES IN SPORTS HISTORY. DURING COLLEGE AT SYRACUSE UNIVERSITY, JIM PLAYED FOOTBALL, LACROSSE, AND BASKETBALL BEFORE DECIDING TO STICK WITH FOOTBALL PROFESSIONALLY. INCREDIBLY, JIM BROWN NEVER MISSED A SINGLE GAME DURING HIS 9-YEAR CAREER, EVEN WITH DEFENSES STACKING UP TO STOP HIM!

RUNNING BACK
WALTER "SWEETNESS" PAYTON

Walter "Sweetness" Payton changed what people came to expect from running backs. He played from 1975 to 1987 and nobody else was nearly as smooth on the field.

When Walter Payton retired he had racked up a total of 16,726 rushing yards, which was the all-time record at the time. (Sweetness was later passed by another great, Emmitt Smith, as the all-time leading rusher.) Not only did Walter Payton move his team down the field, he also completed drives, scoring 125 touchdowns for a total of 750 points.

A RECORD-BREAKING PERFORMANCE

SWEETNESS WAS ESPECIALLY SWEET ONE DAY IN 1977, PLAYING AGAINST THE MINNESOTA VIKINGS. WALTER PAYTON COULD NOT BE STOPPED, SLIDING PAST AND RUNNING RIGHT THROUGH THE VIKINGS' DEFENSE. BY THE END OF THE GAME, PAYTON HAD RUSHED FOR A TOTAL OF 275 YARDS, THE MOST EVER IN A SINGLE GAME AT THAT TIME!

WIDE RECEIVER
JERRY RICE

No other wide receiver has played more than Jerry Rice's 20 seasons from 1985 to 2005. To give an idea of how **dominant** Jerry Rice was, here are the records he holds: career catches (1,549), receiving yards (22,895), and total touchdowns (208). That touchdown record isn't just for wide receivers. It's the all-time record for everybody. No NFL player has scored more touchdowns in his career than Jerry Rice!

But Jerry Rice wasn't just a great individual player. He was an important member of a team. He played with Joe Montana and together their San Francisco 49ers won the Super Bowl three times. A long list of personal records and being part of a winning team are both signs of a truly great player!

MOST PEOPLE REMEMBER JERRY RICE IN THE SAN FRANCISCO 49ERS' RED AND GOLD! RICE DID PLAY MOST OF HIS CAREER WITH THE 49ERS, BUT HE ALSO PLAYED FOR THE SEATTLE SEAHAWKS AND OAKLAND RAIDERS.

FROM THE LEGEND HIMSELF

JERRY RICE SAID OF HIS JOB ON THE FIELD: "I DON'T THINK I'M SUCH A NATURAL. I THINK WHAT I'M DOING IS VERY HARD WORK. I WORK HARD TO KEEP IN SHAPE . . . CORNERBACKS ARE THE BEST ATHLETES ON THE TEAM . . . THOSE ARE THE GUYS I HAVE TO BEAT. IT ISN'T EASY."

TIGHT END
TONY GONZALEZ

When people once thought of offenses in football, they immediately thought about quarterbacks, running backs, and wide receivers. Tony Gonzalez changed that, **redefining** how fans viewed the tight end position forever. On any given play, a tight end could be asked to go out for a pass or block to give the quarterback more time to throw.

Tony Gonzalez did both, and he did them better than nearly anyone else. Gonzalez has the second most catches of all time for any position, not just a tight end. Only Jerry Rice has more. Tony Gonzalez moved the ball 15,127 yards and scored 111 touchdowns in his career.

TONY GONZALEZ PLAYED FOR 17 SEASONS ALTOGETHER. HE WAS WITH THE KANSAS CITY CHIEFS FOR 12 YEARS BEFORE CLOSING HIS CAREER PLAYING 5 YEARS WITH THE ATLANTA FALCONS.

LOVE FOR THE GAME

NOT ONLY WAS TONY GONZALEZ GOOD, HE WAS ALWAYS THERE. TONY ONLY EVER MISSED ONE GAME DURING HIS CAREER, EVEN THOUGH TIGHT END IS ONE OF THE MOST PHYSICALLY DEMANDING POSITIONS IN FOOTBALL. THOUGH HE RETIRED, YOU CAN STILL SEE TONY GONZALEZ ON TV BEFORE GAMES AS A SPORTS **ANALYST**, GIVING HIS VALUABLE THOUGHTS ON CURRENT TEAMS.

OFFENSIVE LINE
ANTHONY MUÑOZ

It's common in football to call the offensive and defensive line the "trenches." Every play is a battle and Anthony Muñoz won many more than he lost. Muñoz was known for being a straight-on blocker, meaning he had to have both the strength and quickness to take defenses on head-to-head.

People don't play on the offensive line for **glamour** and fame. Many fans don't know their names. Instead, these are the men who get in there and get the job done. Muñoz did his job better than most and received the highest honors for offensive linemen. He went to the Pro Bowl, football's all-star game, 11 times in a row!

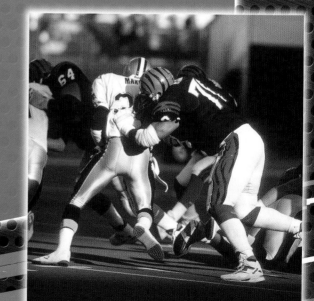

ANTHONY MUÑOZ PLAYED FOR THE CINCINNATI BENGALS AND IS ONE OF THE GREATEST BENGALS EVER. MUÑOZ WAS INDUCTED INTO THE NFL HALL OF FAME IN 1998.

WELCOME TO THE BENGALS' JUNGLE!

AT 6 FEET, 6 INCHES (2 M) AND 278 POUNDS (126 KG), ANTHONY MUÑOZ WAS A BEAST OF A MAN. HE PUT TOGETHER A WEIGHT ROOM IN HIS OWN HOUSE AND WAS KNOWN FOR HIS **DETERMINATION** AND HARD WORK. HE ALSO RAN SEVERAL MILES EVERY SINGLE DAY. GOOD LUCK GETTING PAST SOMEONE LIKE THAT!

DEFENSIVE LINE
REGGIE WHITE

It's about time this book made it to the defensive players! There is no better place to start than with Reggie White, one of the most feared defensive linemen in NFL history. Reggie White won the defensive Rookie of the Year award after his first season. After that, he went to 13 straight Pro Bowls.

There is a famous story that Reggie White would tell his teammates in the huddle before a play that he was going to sack the quarterback . . . and then he would do just what he said he would! When he retired after 15 seasons, Reggie White was the all-time sack leader with 198 sacks.

A "CHEESEHEAD" LEGEND

REGGIE WHITE PLAYED HIS FIRST EIGHT SEASONS WITH THE PHILADELPHIA EAGLES BEFORE BECOMING A GREEN BAY PACKER. THE PACKERS ARE NICKNAMED THE "CHEESEHEADS" BECAUSE OF FANS WEARING CHEESE WEDGE HATS ON THEIR HEADS TO GAMES! REGGIE WON THE SUPER BOWL WITH THE PACKERS IN 1997 AND HAD THREE SACKS IN THE CHAMPIONSHIP GAME.

LINEBACKER
LAWRENCE TAYLOR

If you like football for the hard hits and crushing tackles, then Lawrence Taylor is your man. Taylor played outside linebacker, but had a talent for getting inside the other team's head! He **single-handedly** changed the way his position worked. Defenses expected him to drop back and defend short passes, but he charged straight through to sack the quarterback.

Lawrence Taylor had the speed to run right past offensive linemen and the strength to outmuscle them. Over his entire time playing football, Lawrence Taylor sacked the quarterback over 130 times, made over 1,000 tackles, made his opponents fumble 33 times, and intercepted 9 passes!

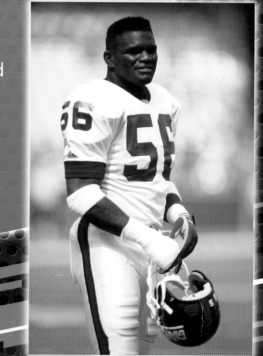

THE NEW YORK GIANTS HAVE NEVER BEEN BETTER THAN WHEN LAWRENCE TAYLOR WAS PLAYING. HE LED THE GIANTS TO THE PLAYOFFS SIX TIMES AND WON TWO SUPER BOWLS.

LAYING DOWN THE LAW-RENCE

ONLY TWO (YES, TWO!) DEFENSIVE PLAYERS HAVE EVER WON THE NFL MVP AWARD AND LAWRENCE TAYLOR IS ONE OF THEM! THE YEAR THAT HE WON, HE HAD 20 SACKS, 105 TACKLES, AND CAUSED 2 FUMBLES. A SEASON IS 16 GAMES, WHICH MEANS HE AVERAGED 6 TACKLES AND AT LEAST ONE SACK EACH GAME.

DEFENSIVE BACK
RONNIE LOTT

Ronnie Lott did a lot! He played four different positions in the 14 seasons he spent in the NFL: both left and right cornerback, free safety, and strong safety. Lott was known for his hard-hitting style. He would either intercept passes or knock the ball right out of the wide receiver's hands.

Good luck trying to catch a pass with Ronnie Lott on his way over! Lott was said to be almost able to see a play before it happened, since he always seemed to be in the perfect position. Overall, Ronnie Lott had over 1,000 tackles and 63 intercepted passes.

RONNIE LOTT IS MOST REMEMBERED AS A SAN FRANCISCO 49ER AND WON FOUR SUPER BOWLS WITH THEM. WEARING THE SAN FRANCISCO GOLD AND RED, HE WAS A HUMAN STOP SIGN FOR **OPPOSING** OFFENSES.

WHO NEEDS 10 FINGERS ANYWAY?

EARLIER IN THIS BOOK, WIDE RECEIVER JERRY RICE SAID THAT CORNERBACKS WERE THE BEST ATHLETES IN FOOTBALL. THIS MAKES SENSE WITH THE WAY RONNIE LOTT PLAYED. HIS TOUGHNESS BECAME FAMOUS WHEN HE SMASHED HIS PINKY FINGER DURING A GAME. RATHER THAN STOP PLAYING, HE ACTUALLY CUT OFF THE TOP PART OF HIS PINKY TO KEEP GOING!

FUTURE RECORD
BREAKERS

There you have it! You have now learned about the accuracy and leadership of quarterbacks, speed of running backs, hands of receivers, power of linemen, and hits of the defense. These are the greatest NFL football players of all time! Who seemed most interesting to you?

There are many more legendary players, stories, and teams to explore. Football is a sport with an interesting history. If you would like to know more, ask a coach, check out a book from the library, or tune in to games on the radio, TV, or in person!

AARON RODGERS HAS BEEN A QUARTERBACK FOR THE GREEN BAY PACKERS SINCE 2005. HE HAS WON A SUPER BOWL AND BEEN NAMED MVP OF THE LEAGUE TWO TIMES. RODGERS ONCE THREW 402 CONSECUTIVE PASSES WITHOUT AN INTERCEPTION.

FUTURE HALL OF FAMERS

PLAYER & TEAM	POSITION	WHAT MAKES THEM GREAT?
PEYTON MANNING INDIANAPOLIS COLTS	QUARTERBACK	MOST CAREER TOUCHDOWN PASSES (539) 2ND MOST CAREER PASSING YARDS (71,940) MOST TOUCHDOWNS IN ONE SEASON (55)
TOM BRADY* NEW ENGLAND PATRIOTS	QUARTERBACK	MADE IT TO THE SUPER BOWL 9 TIMES WON THE SUPER BOWL 6 TIMES
DREW BREES* NEW ORLEANS SAINTS	QUARTERBACK	MOST CAREER PASSING YARDS (74,437)
ADRIAN PETERSON* MINNESOTA VIKINGS	RUNNING BACK	MOST RUSHING YARDS IN A SINGLE GAME (296) 8TH MOST RUSHING YARDS OF ALL TIME
LARRY FITZGERALD* ARIZONA CARDINALS	WIDE RECEIVER	2ND MOST RECEIVING YARDS OF ALL TIME
CALVIN JOHNSON DETROIT LIONS	WIDE RECEIVER	MOST RECEIVING YARDS IN A SINGLE SEASON (1,964)
JOE THOMAS CLEVELAND BROWNS	OFFENSIVE LINE	PLAYED THE MOST PLAYS IN A ROW IN NFL HISTORY (10,363 PLAYS WITHOUT TAKING ONE OFF)
JULIUS PEPPERS CAROLINA PANTHERS	DEFENSIVE LINE	4TH MOST SACKS IN NFL HISTORY
RICHARD SHERMAN* SEATTLE SEAHAWKS	DEFENSIVE BACK	KNOWN FOR HIS CONFIDENT ATTITUDE AND TRASH TALK 4 PRO BOWLS AND HAS WON THE SUPER BOWL
EARL THOMAS* SEATTLE SEAHAWKS	SAFETY	ONE OF THE MOST FEARED SAFETIES IN THE NFL TODAY 6 PRO BOWLS AND WON THE SUPER BOWL
STEPHEN GOSTKOWSKI* NEW ENGLAND PATRIOTS	KICKER	MOST EXTRA POINTS IN A ROW IN NFL HISTORY

*PLAYER IS STILL PLAYING AS OF 2019. STATS THROUGH 2018–2019 SEASON

THE NEXT NFL LEGEND?

WHAT ISN'T WRITTEN DOWN IN RECORD BOOKS IS THE HOURS OF PRACTICING, LEARNING, AND STUDYING THAT EACH OF THESE PLAYERS DID TO BECOME SUCCESSFUL. THE BEST WAY TO GET BETTER AT SOMETHING IS TO ENJOY IT AND TO DO IT! FIND A FRIEND OR TWO, GRAB A FOOTBALL, GET OUT THERE, AND GO PLAY!

GLOSSARY

analyst: a person who studies or analyzes something

asset: a valuable person or thing

dedication: special faithfulness

determination: the act of deciding something firmly

dominant: the most powerful or strongest

elevation: height above sea level

exceed: to be greater or more than something

fortunate: having good luck

glamour: fashionable appeal

opposing: fighting or competing against another person or group

redefine: define again, or differently

retire: to stop working at your job, either because of age, injury, or personal decision

scramble: when the quarterback runs with the ball while being chased by defensive players

single-handedly: done by one person

FOR MORE INFORMATION

BOOKS

Doeden, Matt. *Play Football Like a Pro: Key Skills and Tips.* Mankato, MN: Capstone Press, 2010.

Jacobs, Greg. *The Everything Kids' Football Book: All-time Greats, Legendary Teams, and Today's Favorite Players—with Tips on Playing Like a Pro.* Avon, MA: Adams Media, 2016.

Sports Illustrated Kids. *1st and 10: Top 10 Lists of Everything in Football.* New York, NY: Sports Illustrated Kids, 2016.

WEBSITES

Learn All About the Sport: Football
www.ducksters.com/sports/football.php
This website has links to learn the rules of football, how each position works, and videos about throwing, tackling, and blocking.

NFL Play 60 Challenge
aha-nflplay60challenge.org/
NFL Play 60 is a program that encourages kids to share their love for sports and physically active lifestyles.

SI Kids: Sports News for Kids, Kids Games and More
www.sikids.com/
This is an all-around great sports resource for kids and includes scores of current games, bios of successful young athletes, and tons of stats, standings, and schedules.

INDEX